PATRICK H. PERRINE

Future Focused

Mastering Tech and Innovation for the Entrepreneur in the Evolving Business World

amazonkindle

DEDICATION

To the visionaries and change-makers who see beyond the horizon: This book is dedicated to you. May it illuminate your path as you harness technology and innovation to craft a better tomorrow for communities worldwide.

Warmly,
Patrick

"I will not have my life narrowed down. I will not bow down to somebody else's whim or to someone else's ignorance."

— BELL HOOKS

Contents

Preface

Welcome to 'Future Focused: Mastering Tech and Innovation for the Entrepreneur in the Evolving Business World,' your essential guide to navigating the forefront of technology and innovation as outlined in Step 9 of 'Unicorn Rising.' As the latest installment in the 'Be A Unicorn' series, this volume dives deeper into the transformative power of technology, offering a comprehensive and actionable exploration of the digital landscape that every entrepreneur must conquer.

In an era where technology reshapes every facet of business, 'Future Focused' serves not only as a guide but as a practical workbook. It is filled with exercises, case studies, and strategies designed to bring the insights of emerging technologies directly into the fabric of your venture. This book aims to transform theoretical knowledge into actionable wisdom, enabling you to harness the full potential of innovations such as AI, IoT, blockchain, and AR/VR for entrepreneurial triumph.

Building upon the foundation set by 'Unicorn Rising' and previous volumes in the 'Be A Unicorn' series, 'Future Focused' reinforces the series' commitment to providing an in-depth, step-by-step education for entrepreneurs. It is meticulously crafted to ensure a seamless progression in your understanding of how to integrate cutting-edge technologies into your business model for sustained growth and competitive advantage.

I invite you to engage with this book actively, applying its lessons to navigate the tech-driven nuances of the modern business environment. Through 'Future Focused,' you will not only grasp the essence of each technological trend but also learn how to apply these innovations strategically to propel your business forward.

'Future Focused' is more than a book; it's a roadmap to mastering the dynamic world of technology and innovation. As you venture through its pages, be prepared to challenge your assumptions, ignite your creativity, and redefine what is possible for your entrepreneurial journey.

Let us embark on this journey to the future of entrepreneurship, where technology and innovation are not just trends to observe but powerful tools to wield. With 'Future Focused,' you are setting sail towards a horizon brimming with limitless possibilities, ready to master the technologies that will define the next era of business success.

Be A Unicorn: The New Entrepreneur's Ultimate Guide To Success

Dream It, Build It:
An Aspirational Odyssey Through
Entrepreneurship in Ten Inspiring Volumes.

Volume Nine

FUTURE FOCUSED
Mastering Tech and Innovation for the Entrepreneur
in the Evolving Business World

1

The Evolving Technological Landscape

"Digital technology allows us a much larger scope to tell stories that were pretty much the grounds of the literary media."
— George Lucas

I n the unfolding narrative of the 21st century, the role of technology emerges as both a catalyst and an arena for unprecedented transformation. This pivotal chapter unfolds the intricate narrative of technological evolution, spotlighting its profound implications for entrepreneurs eager to chart a course through the ever-shifting terrain of the digital age. With a focus on emerging technologies and their potential to redefine market paradigms, this exploration is not merely about adaptation but about strategic foresight and innovation that can set the stage for enduring success.

At the forefront of this technological renaissance are advancements that promise to reshape not only how businesses operate but also how they interact with their customers and compete in the global marketplace. From blockchain's promise

1

of transparency and security to AI's ability to personalize customer experiences and analyze data with unparalleled depth, the opportunities for entrepreneurial ingenuity are boundless. This chapter serves as a guide for navigating these opportunities, offering insights into leveraging cutting-edge technologies to enhance operational efficiency, drive customer engagement, and foster a culture of continuous innovation.

Moreover, this journey into the evolving technological landscape emphasizes the importance of a visionary mindset and agile approach. It challenges entrepreneurs to look beyond the horizon, to not only keep pace with technological advancements but to anticipate and shape them. Through real-world anecdotes, strategic frameworks, and practical exercises, entrepreneurs are equipped to harness the power of technology not just as a tool for solving existing problems but as a foundation for creating new possibilities and achieving competitive advantage.

Opening Anecdote: Netflix's Visionary Leap

In the late 1990s, Reed Hastings and Marc Randolph co-founded Netflix, initially as a DVD rental service. However, it was their early and bold bet on streaming technology that catapulted Netflix from a mail-order service to a global streaming powerhouse. Their foresight into the digital revolution redefined entertainment, illustrating the transformative power of embracing technological advancements.

Quick Thought:

Innovation is not just about adopting new technologies; it's about foreseeing change and positioning your venture to ride the wave, rather than be engulfed by it.

Entrepreneurship in Action: Key Ingredients

- **Visionary Thinking:** Look beyond the current trends and anticipate the next big wave in technology.
- **Agility:** Be prepared to pivot and adapt your business model in response to new technological developments.
- **Persistent Learning:** Commit to ongoing education and exploration in the tech space to keep your business at the cutting edge.

Case Study: SpaceX's Reusability Revolution

Background: SpaceX, led by Elon Musk, embarked on a mission to reduce space travel costs and make Mars colonization feasible. A pivotal aspect of this vision was the development of reusable rocket technology, a stark departure from the traditional single-use rockets. This initiative aimed to revolutionize space travel by drastically lowering costs and increasing launch frequency.

Approach: SpaceX's approach was marked by relentless innovation and resilience in the face of failures. The company's engineers and scientists conducted extensive research and development to create rockets that could land back on Earth after launch. This journey involved numerous tests, some resulting in explosive failures, but each providing valuable data to refine their technology.

Solution: The culmination of these efforts was the successful landing of the Falcon 9 rocket's first stage on a drone ship in 2016. This breakthrough demonstrated the feasibility of reusable rockets, marking a significant milestone in aerospace history. SpaceX continued to iterate on this technology, achieving multiple successful landings and re-flights of the Falcon 9 first stage, thus validating the concept of reusability.

Impact: SpaceX's reusable rockets have not only reduced the cost of access to space but also increased the pace of space exploration. This innovation has catalyzed the industry, with other companies and space agencies exploring reusable technologies. SpaceX's achievements have opened up new possibilities for satellite deployment, International Space Station resupply missions, and interplanetary travel.

Legacy and Insights: SpaceX's journey underscores the transformative power of perseverance, innovation, and visionary leadership in overcoming technical challenges. The company's success with reusable rockets stands as a testament to the potential of rethinking established norms and pushing the boundaries of what is possible. This case study exemplifies the impact of disruptive technology on an industry, setting new standards and inspiring a new generation of exploration and innovation.

Pro Tip: Stay curious. The willingness to explore and understand emerging technologies can uncover opportunities that might otherwise go unnoticed.

Exercise: Technology Adoption and Innovation Challenge

1. Technology Trend Analysis:

- **Research and Identify:** Select three cutting-edge technologies that could impact your industry in the next five years. Resources might include tech journals, innovation blogs, and industry reports.
- **Analyze Implications:** For each technology, write a brief analysis on its potential implications for your business or sector, focusing on opportunities and challenges.
- **Strategic Implications:** Discuss how these technologies could alter the competitive landscape and how your business might adapt or lead in this new environment.

2. Innovative Application Workshop:

- **Ideation Session:** Based on the technologies identified, conduct an ideation session to brainstorm potential applications within your business. Encourage radical thinking and diverse perspectives.
- **Concept Development:** Choose the most promising idea and develop a concept note outlining the solution, target market, and value proposition.
- **Feasibility Study:** Perform a preliminary feasibility study to assess the practicality, required resources, and potential impact of the proposed solution.

3. Prototype and Feedback Loop:

- **Rapid Prototyping:** Create a simple prototype or mockup of your solution. This could range from a software demo to a physical product model, depending on the nature of the idea.
- **Feedback Collection:** Present your prototype to a small group of potential users, stakeholders, or industry experts. Collect feedback on usability, desirability, and viability.
- **Iterate and Refine:** Based on the feedback, iterate on your prototype. This process may involve several rounds of refinement to hone the solution and better meet user needs and market demands.

Challenge For You:

Embrace a technology or innovation that seems out of reach or futuristic for your current business model. Develop a strategic plan to explore this technology, including potential partnerships, R&D investments, or pilot projects. Reflect on how this exercise shifts your perspective on innovation and long-term planning.

Conclusion:

This chapter serves as your compass in the vast ocean of technological advancements. By understanding and leveraging the currents of change, entrepreneurs can not only survive but thrive. The journey through the evolving technological landscape is fraught with challenges but rich with opportunities. As we continue to explore each technological trend in the upcoming chapters, remember that the future belongs to those who are prepared to embrace change, innovate, and lead the charge into the new digital era.

Let's embark on this journey together, with our sights set

on the horizon, ready to harness the power of technology to illuminate the path to entrepreneurial success.

2

Digital Transformation and its Implications

"Digital technology provides a low-cost way for people all over the world to get more access to information, more opportunities to speak and hear, and more freedom to express their views."
— Bill Gates

I n an age where digital innovation becomes the linch-pin of competitive advantage, the journey of digital transformation is no longer optional but imperative for businesses seeking to thrive. This chapter delves deep into the essence of digital transformation, exploring its vast potential to revolutionize how businesses operate, engage with customers, and innovate in an increasingly interconnected world. It's a narrative that transcends technological adoption, focusing on a holistic reshaping of organizational cultures, processes, and strategies to leverage digital advancements effectively.

The essence of digital transformation lies in its ability to reimagine the business in the context of an ever-evolving digital landscape. It's about creating a dynamic ecosystem where digital technologies are not merely adjuncts to business operations but integral components driving growth, efficiency, and customer satisfaction. This transformation demands a shift in mindset, from viewing technology as a support function to embracing it as a core strategic pillar, capable of unlocking new business models, markets, and opportunities for value creation.

At the heart of successful digital transformation is the understanding that this endeavor is about more than just technology—it's about people, processes, and purpose. It requires a concerted effort to align technology with business goals, fostering an environment where innovation flourishes, and digital tools empower employees to deliver exceptional value to customers. Through illustrative examples, practical strategies, and actionable insights, this chapter aims to guide entrepreneurs on their journey towards achieving a seamless digital transformation, highlighting the critical role of leadership, culture, and customer-centricity in this process.

Opening Anecdote: Amazon's Retail Revolution

Jeff Bezos' Amazon began as an online bookstore but quickly evolved into the world's largest online retailer, fundamentally changing shopping habits. Amazon's success is a testament to digital transformation, leveraging technology to offer unparalleled customer convenience, personalized experiences, and a seemingly endless product range. Their use of big data, cloud computing, and AI to predict customer preferences and streamline logistics has set new standards for retail and customer service.

Quick Thought:

Digital transformation is more than a technological upgrade; it's a strategic realignment of a company's operations and vision to thrive in the digital age.

Entrepreneurship in Action: Key Ingredients

- **Customer-Centricity:** Use digital tools to understand and anticipate the needs of your customers better.
- **Agility:** Adapt quickly to technological advancements and market changes.
- **Innovation:** Continuously seek ways to use technology to improve products, processes, and business models.

Case Study: Zara's Fast Fashion Onslaught

Background: Zara, a flagship brand of the Inditex Group, stands out in the fast fashion industry for its unique business model that blends fashion with technology. Its approach to digital transformation focuses on speed, efficiency, and responsiveness to fashion trends.

Approach: Zara leverages advanced data analytics and AI to track customer preferences and fast-moving trends. Their supply chain is highly automated, from production to distribution, enabling rapid design, manufacture, and delivery of new clothing to stores worldwide in as little as two weeks.

Solution: Implementing an integrated online-offline store experience, Zara uses technology to enhance customer shopping experiences, offering features like real-time inventory tracking, online order in-store pickups, and fast checkout processes.

Impact: Zara's digital transformation has not only cemented its position as a leader in fast fashion but also redefined expectations around the retail experience. They've achieved remarkable agility, trend responsiveness, and customer loyalty, outpacing competitors and setting new industry benchmarks.

Legacy and Insights: Zara's success story underscores the importance of integrating digital technologies across all business facets to remain competitive. It highlights how businesses can use digital transformation to streamline operations, respond quickly to market changes, and deliver exceptional customer experiences.

> Pro Tip: Embrace Change as a Constant: Digital transformation is not a one-time project but an ongoing journey of adaptation and growth. Cultivate a culture within your organization that views change as an opportunity rather than a threat. This mindset will empower your team to innovate continuously, adapt to new technologies swiftly, and stay ahead in a digitally evolving landscape.

Exercise: Digital Transformation Blueprint

1. Digital Audit and Vision Crafting:

- **Current State Analysis:** Conduct a comprehensive audit of your current digital capabilities and identify gaps.

- **Vision Statement:** Craft a vision statement that defines what digital transformation means for your business and outlines the ultimate objectives of this transformation.
- **Stakeholder Engagement:** Involve key stakeholders in the vision crafting process to ensure alignment and buy-in across the organization.

2. Strategy Development and Implementation Planning:

- **Strategic Goals Setting:** Define specific, measurable goals that align with your digital transformation vision.
- **Implementation Roadmap:** Create a detailed implementation roadmap with timelines, milestones, and responsible parties for each initiative.
- **Resource Allocation:** Determine the resources (financial, human, technological) required for each initiative and plan accordingly.

3. Execution, Monitoring, and Continuous Improvement:

- **Kick-off Initiatives:** Begin executing according to the roadmap, focusing on quick wins to build momentum.
- **Performance Monitoring:** Regularly track progress against goals using key performance indicators (KPIs) and adjust strategies as necessary.
- **Iterative Improvement:** Foster a culture of continuous learning and improvement, using feedback and data to refine and enhance digital initiatives.

Challenge For You:

Identify a process within your business that is currently

manual and time-consuming. Design a digital solution to automate this process, considering the tools, technologies, and strategies you would need to implement it. Reflect on how this change could improve efficiency, customer satisfaction, or product quality.

Conclusion:

This chapter has laid out the framework for understanding and navigating the complexities of digital transformation. By examining the principles underlying successful transformations and providing actionable strategies, we aim to equip entrepreneurs with the knowledge to not only survive but thrive in the digital age. As we progress, remember that digital transformation is a continuous journey, requiring constant adaptation, learning, and growth. Let's embrace this journey with open minds and innovative spirits, ready to transform challenges into opportunities for unprecedented success.

3

Artificial Intelligence and Machine Learning

"The real question is, when will we draft an artificial intelligence bill of rights? What will that consist of? And who will get to decide that?"
— Gray Scott

I n the vortex of today's rapidly evolving technological landscape, Artificial Intelligence (AI) and Machine Learning (ML) emerge not just as buzzwords but as pillars of innovation that can redefine the trajectory of entrepreneurial ventures. This chapter endeavors to peel back the layers of complexity surrounding AI and ML, illuminating their transformative capabilities across various facets of business from operational optimization to customer engagement and beyond. It's a narrative that underscores the duality of AI and ML as both disruptors and enablers, charting a path for entrepreneurs to harness these technologies in crafting ventures that are not only economically successful but also technologically avant-garde.

As we delve into the core of AI and ML, we uncover their potential to act as catalysts for deep-seated change, enabling businesses to leapfrog traditional constraints and unlock new realms of possibility. The essence of leveraging AI and ML lies in their capacity to distill insights from data at a scale and speed unattainable to human cognition, offering businesses an unparalleled advantage in understanding and predicting market dynamics, consumer behavior, and even the innovation lifecycle itself. This chapter aims to equip entrepreneurs with the insights and tools to strategically deploy AI and ML, transforming these technologies from mere concepts into integral components of their business strategy.

Central to this discussion is the recognition of the ethical and societal implications of AI and ML deployment. As we explore the vast potential of these technologies, we also pause to consider the responsibility that comes with their use. It's about striking a balance between innovation and integrity, ensuring that the pursuit of technological advancement does not eclipse the core values of equity, transparency, and human welfare. Through a blend of theoretical exploration, practical application, and ethical contemplation, this chapter offers a comprehensive overview of AI and ML's role in sculpting the future of entrepreneurship.

Opening Anecdote: IBM Watson's Healthcare Breakthroughs

IBM's Watson, an AI system capable of answering questions posed in natural language, has been a pioneer in leveraging AI for healthcare. Watson's ability to sift through vast amounts of medical data has enhanced diagnostic accuracy, personalized patient care, and revolutionized the healthcare industry's approach to combating complex diseases. This example illustrates the profound impact AI can have on improving lives and operational efficiency.

> ***Quick Thought:***
> *AI and ML are not just about technology; they're about envisioning a future where decisions are more informed, processes are more efficient, and experiences are deeply personalized.*

Entrepreneurship in Action: Key Ingredients

- **Data Mastery:** The lifeblood of AI and ML; understanding and leveraging the right data can unveil patterns and opportunities invisible to the human eye.
- **Innovative Mindset:** Constantly seeking novel applications for AI and ML that can disrupt traditional business models or create new market niches.
- **Ethical Consideration:** Navigating the power of AI with a strong ethical compass to ensure technology serves humanity positively.

Case Study: DeepMind's Game-Changing AI Research

Background: DeepMind, a subsidiary of Alphabet Inc., has been at the cutting edge of AI research, developing systems that can learn and excel at a variety of tasks, from defeating world champions in the game of Go to advancing scientific discoveries.

Approach: DeepMind's approach involves developing AI that can learn from vast amounts of data using neural networks, a method inspired by the human brain's structure. This enables their AI to understand complex patterns and make decisions with a level of intuition akin to human cognition.

Solution: One of DeepMind's notable achievements is AlphaFold, an AI that predicts the 3D shapes of proteins, crucial for understanding biological life and developing new medicines. AlphaFold's accuracy in predicting protein structures has been heralded as a significant breakthrough in the field of biology.

Impact: DeepMind's work illustrates AI's potential to solve problems previously deemed insurmountable, opening new avenues for scientific research, medical advancements, and beyond. It demonstrates how AI and ML can extend human capability and drive progress in ways that were unimaginable just a few years ago.

Legacy and Insights: The legacy of DeepMind's innovations is a testament to the transformative power of AI and ML when applied with creativity and rigor. It challenges entrepreneurs to think big and consider how AI can be used to address complex global challenges.

```
Pro Tip: Leverage IoT Data for Insights: The true
value of IoT lies not just in the connectivity of
devices but in the data they generate. Implement
robust analytics to turn this data into actionable
insights. This could mean predictive maintenance for
manufacturing equipment, personalized experiences for
retail customers, or efficiency improvements in
energy usage. By translating IoT data into business
intelligence, you can make more informed decisions,
optimize operations, and create innovative services
that meet your customers' evolving needs.
```

Exercise: AI and ML Innovation Workshop

1. Ideation and Opportunity Identification:

- **Market Needs Analysis:** Investigate and identify pressing problems or unmet needs within your industry that AI and ML could address.
- **Brainstorming Session:** Organize a brainstorming session to generate innovative AI/ML solution ideas for identified problems.
- **Opportunity Evaluation:** Assess the feasibility, market potential, and impact of the proposed solutions.

2. Development and Prototyping:

- **Skills and Tools Assessment:** Determine the skills and tools required to develop your AI/ML solution. Consider partnerships or external expertise if necessary.
- **Prototype Development:** Develop a minimum viable

product (MVP) or prototype to test your solution in a real-world environment.

- **Feedback and Iteration:** Collect feedback from users and stakeholders, and iteratively refine your solution based on this feedback.

3. Implementation and Scaling:

- **Go-to-Market Strategy:** Develop a comprehensive strategy for launching your AI/ML solution, considering market entry, target audience, and scaling.
- **Impact Assessment:** Regularly assess the impact of your solution on your business and the broader industry, adjusting your strategy as needed for maximum effect.
- **Continuous Learning:** Stay abreast of the latest AI/ML developments and continuously explore ways to integrate new advancements into your solution.

Challenge For You:

Imagine a future where your entrepreneurial venture has successfully integrated AI and ML into every facet of its operations. Sketch out what this future looks like, how it has transformed your business, and the broader societal impacts. Reflect on the steps needed to turn this vision into reality.

Conclusion:

As we've explored in this chapter, AI and ML offer a canvas for innovation, efficiency, and transformation. By understanding their capabilities, potential applications, and the ethical landscape, entrepreneurs can harness these technologies to forge ahead in the competitive business world. The journey into AI and ML is one of exploration, learning, and ethical consideration, poised to redefine the boundaries of what's possible in business and beyond.

Let this chapter serve as a springboard into the profound world of AI and ML, inspiring you to envision and create a future where technology amplifies human potential and drives meaningful progress.

4

Internet of Things (IoT) and Connectivity

"The Internet of Things has the potential to change the world, just as the Internet did. Maybe even more so."
— Kevin Ashton

In an age where connectivity is almost as essential as the air we breathe, the Internet of Things (IoT) has emerged as a transformative force, reshaping the landscape of countless industries and redefining the essence of innovation. The concept of IoT extends the power of the internet beyond computers and smartphones to a broad range of environments and objects, creating a network of interconnected devices that communicate and interact with each other. This chapter ventures into the heart of IoT and connectivity, illuminating their pivotal roles in fostering a new era of smart solutions and operational efficiency that can catapult entrepreneurial ventures to unprecedented heights.

IoT's ability to bridge the physical and digital worlds opens up a plethora of opportunities for entrepreneurs to innovate in ways that were once thought to be the realm of science fiction. From smart homes and cities to precision agriculture and beyond, IoT connectivity unlocks the potential to not only streamline operations but also to create deeply personalized customer experiences and sustainable solutions. This chapter seeks to demystify the complexities of IoT, offering a roadmap for entrepreneurs to leverage this technology in creating smarter, more responsive ventures that can adapt to the ever-evolving demands of the digital age.

At the core of IoT's transformative power is the ability to collect, analyze, and act upon data in real-time, providing a foundation for making informed decisions, predicting future trends, and crafting experiences that resonate on a personal level with consumers. However, the journey of integrating IoT into entrepreneurial ventures is fraught with challenges, from ensuring data privacy and security to navigating the intricacies of device interoperability. This chapter aims to equip entrepreneurs with the knowledge and strategies to navigate these challenges, harnessing the full potential of IoT and connectivity to drive innovation, efficiency, and growth.

Opening Anecdote: Revolutionizing Hospitality with Airbnb's Smart Integration

Joe Gebbia and Brian Chesky, the co-founders of Airbnb, harnessed IoT to enhance their platform's user experience, offering smart locks and thermostats to hosts for better guest convenience. This integration of IoT not only simplified the check-in and stay experience but also underscored the potential of IoT to add value in the sharing economy, setting a new standard for hospitality in the digital age.

Quick Thought:
  IoT's essence lies in its ability to turn ordinary objects into sources of data and insights, opening a myriad of opportunities for businesses to innovate and serve their customers better.

Entrepreneurship in Action: Key Ingredients

- **Strategic Connectivity:** Leveraging IoT to create a network of interconnected devices, offering seamless experiences and insights.
- **Data-Driven Decision Making:** Utilizing the rich data from IoT devices to inform strategic decisions, optimize operations, and personalize customer experiences.
- **Innovation and Adaptability:** Continuously exploring new IoT applications to stay ahead in a rapidly evolving technological landscape.

Case Study: Philips Hue and the Smart Lighting Revolution

Background: Philips Hue represents a pioneering success in the smart home industry, offering a range of IoT-enabled lighting products that users can control via their smartphones, voice commands, or integration with other smart home systems.

Approach: By embedding IoT capabilities into lighting products, Philips Hue has transformed how people interact with light. The system allows users to adjust brightness, change colors, and set schedules, enhancing both the functionality and ambiance of living spaces.

Solution: The success of Philips Hue lies in its ecosystem approach, combining intuitive apps, a robust range of products, and compatibility with other smart home technologies, creating a seamless user experience that extends beyond simple illumination.

Impact: Philips Hue not only pioneered smart lighting but also contributed to the broader adoption of IoT in homes, demonstrating how connectivity can enrich everyday life. Its success showcases the potential for IoT to create new user experiences and open up new markets for entrepreneurs.

```
Pro Tip: Innovation Through Integration: The success
of an IoT project often hinges on how well it
integrates with existing systems and enhances the
user experience. Focus on solutions that blend
seamlessly into users' lives, providing utility and
value without complication. Consider how IoT can not
only solve current problems but also anticipate
future needs, setting your venture apart as a leader
in innovation.
```

Challenges and Considerations in IoT Implementation

Data Security and Privacy:

As IoT devices proliferate, so do the risks associated with data breaches and privacy violations. Entrepreneurs must prioritize robust security measures to protect user data and maintain trust.

Interoperability and Standards:
The diversity of IoT devices and protocols poses challenges for interoperability. Entrepreneurs should advocate for and adhere to industry standards to ensure devices can seamlessly communicate and integrate.

Scalability and Infrastructure:
Effective IoT solutions require scalable infrastructure to handle the data volume and connectivity demands. Planning for scalability from the outset is crucial for long-term success.

Exercise: IoT Innovation Sprint

1. Opportunity Identification:

- **Market Research:** Conduct research to identify unmet needs or inefficiencies in your target market that IoT could address.
- **Idea Generation:** Host a brainstorming session to develop innovative IoT solution concepts that meet these needs.
- **Feasibility Analysis:** Evaluate the technical and economic feasibility of your top ideas, considering factors like market demand, development cost, and potential ROI.

2. Prototype and Validation:

- **Rapid Prototyping:** Develop a functional prototype of your IoT solution using lean methodologies to quickly bring your concept to life.
- **User Testing:** Conduct user testing with a small, representative segment of your target market to gather feedback on usability, value, and potential improvements.

- **Iterative Refinement:** Use the feedback to refine your prototype, focusing on enhancing user experience and value proposition.

3. Launch and Scale:

- **Go-to-Market Strategy:** Develop a comprehensive go-to-market strategy that outlines how you will launch, market, and sell your IoT solution.
- **Scaling Plan:** Create a plan for scaling your solution, considering infrastructure, supply chain, and customer support needs as you grow.
- **Continuous Improvement:** Establish mechanisms for ongoing feedback and iteration, ensuring your solution remains relevant and competitive.

Challenge For You:

Envision a future where your entrepreneurial venture has fully integrated IoT solutions, transforming your operations, products, or services. Outline the steps and challenges in achieving this vision, considering the impact on your business model, customer experience, and industry landscape.

Conclusion:

IoT and connectivity offer a frontier of opportunities for entrepreneurs willing to explore and innovate. By understanding IoT's potential, navigating its challenges, and leveraging its capabilities, entrepreneurs can unlock new efficiencies, create novel products and services, and redefine industries. As we continue to witness the expansion of IoT, it's clear that its impact will be profound and far-reaching, heralding a new era of connectivity and innovation.

The journey through IoT is just beginning. Let this chapter inspire you to explore the possibilities and lead the charge in harnessing the power of IoT for a smarter, more connected world.

5

Blockchain and Distributed Ledger Technology

"Blockchain is the tech. Bitcoin is merely the first mainstream manifestation of its potential."
— Marc Andreessen

Venturing into the realm of blockchain and Distributed Ledger Technology (DLT) unveils a future where digital trust and transparency are not just ideals, but foundational pillars of business operations. This chapter ventures into the dynamic realms of blockchain and Distributed Ledger Technology (DLT), illuminating their roles as harbingers of a new digital epoch marked by innovation, trust, and a reimagined approach to digital transactions. By dissecting blockchain's core principles, multifaceted applications, and its sweeping implications, we pave a path for entrepreneurs to navigate and leverage this technology in sculpting ventures that are not only at the technological vanguard but also epitomes of transparency and efficiency.

As we delve into the intricate tapestry of blockchain and DLT, we uncover their unparalleled potential in catalyzing change, streamlining processes, and fostering an environment where trust is not just an expectation but a guarantee. This exploration is not merely about understanding a technology but about envisioning a future where businesses operate on principles of decentralization, security, and indisputable authenticity. Herein lies a guide for entrepreneurs to harness blockchain technology, transforming it from a concept of intrigue into a cornerstone of their business strategy, driving innovation and integrity in equal measure.

Moreover, this chapter considers the ethical dimensions and societal impacts of widespread blockchain adoption. It underscores the imperative of wielding this powerful technology with a conscientious approach, ensuring that its deployment benefits society at large and contributes to the establishment of equitable digital ecosystems. Through a comprehensive exploration that intertwines theory with practical applications, this narrative aims to equip entrepreneurs with a deep understanding of blockchain and DLT's transformative potential, inspiring them to embrace these technologies in crafting a future that is secure, transparent, and boundlessly innovative.

Opening Anecdote: De Beers' Diamond Traceability

De Beers, the world's leading diamond company, has leveraged blockchain technology to ensure the ethical sourcing and authenticity of its diamonds. Through its Tracr platform, every diamond's journey from mine to retail is securely recorded on the blockchain, providing unprecedented transparency and trust in the diamond industry. This initiative showcases how blockchain can transform traditional practices into secure, transparent, and ethical operations.

> ### *Quick Thought:*
> *Blockchain's essence lies in its ability to foster trust in digital transactions, making it a foundational technology for the future of secure, decentralized business operations.*

Entrepreneurship in Action: Key Ingredients

- **Transparency:** Leveraging blockchain to create transparent systems where transactions are immutable and verifiable by all parties.
- **Innovation:** Exploring blockchain's potential to redefine business models, streamline operations, and create new market opportunities.
- **Collaboration:** Building partnerships within blockchain ecosystems to enhance trust, interoperability, and collective growth.

Case Study: Estonia's Digital Governance

Background:

Estonia has been a forerunner in adopting blockchain technology for enhancing its digital governance. The country's e-Residency program allows global citizens to start and manage a business in Estonia digitally, with blockchain securing citizens' data and ensuring the integrity of digital transactions.

Approach:

By integrating blockchain into its digital infrastructure,

Estonia has created a highly secure, efficient, and transparent governmental operation system. This approach has streamlined processes, reduced bureaucracy, and enhanced citizen trust in digital services.

Solution:

Estonia's blockchain-based solutions cover a wide array of services, including identity management, health records, and business registration, setting a benchmark for digital governance worldwide.

Impact:

Estonia's pioneering digital governance model demonstrates blockchain's potential to enhance the efficiency, security, and transparency of public services. It serves as a blueprint for other nations and entrepreneurs looking to harness blockchain for secure, decentralized operations.

```
Pro Tip: Start with Trust: When integrating
blockchain into your venture, focus on building trust
with your users. Transparency, security, and user
control over data should be the cornerstones of your
blockchain strategy. By prioritizing trust, you not
only adhere to blockchain's core principles but also
enhance user engagement and loyalty.
```

Exercise: Blockchain Innovation Challenge

1. Ideation and Exploration:

- **Research:** Dive into blockchain's latest trends and developments. Identify how these innovations could be applied within your industry or venture.

- **Problem Identification:** Pinpoint challenges within your business or industry that blockchain could solve, focusing on areas like transparency, efficiency, or security.
- **Solution Brainstorming:** Generate ideas on how blockchain could address these challenges. Consider both direct applications and more innovative, out-of-the-box solutions.

2. Prototype Development:

- **Select a Concept:** Choose the most promising idea from your brainstorming session. Ensure it aligns with your business goals and has the potential for tangible impact.
- **Build a Prototype:** Develop a basic prototype of your blockchain solution. This could be a smart contract, a blockchain-based app, or a tokenization model.
- **Test and Refine:** Conduct initial testing of your prototype. Gather feedback and iterate on the design to improve functionality and user experience.

3. Implementation and Scaling:

- **Develop a Roll-out Strategy:** Plan for the broader implementation of your blockchain solution. Consider technical, operational, and market readiness aspects.
- **Partnerships and Ecosystems:** Explore partnerships with blockchain platforms, service providers, and other stakeholders to enhance your solution's capabilities and reach.

- **Monitor and Adapt:** After launch, continuously monitor your blockchain solution's performance. Be prepared to adapt and evolve your approach based on user feedback and technological advancements.

Challenge For You:

Consider an existing process within your venture that could benefit from enhanced trust and transparency. Design a blockchain solution to reimagine this process, detailing how it would work, the benefits it would offer, and the steps needed to implement it. Reflect on how this solution could transform your venture's operations and stakeholder relationships.

Conclusion:

This chapter has unfolded the transformative potential of blockchain and DLT across various domains, highlighting their role in building trust, enhancing transparency, and fostering innovation. By understanding blockchain's capabilities and integrating them thoughtfully into entrepreneurial ventures, businesses can unlock new efficiencies, create secure and transparent operations, and pave the way for innovative services and products.

As we continue to explore the impact of emerging technologies on entrepreneurship, blockchain stands out as a key enabler of the next generation of digital solutions. Let this chapter inspire you to consider how blockchain can be woven into the fabric of your entrepreneurial journey, driving forward a future where digital trust and decentralization are paramount.

6

Augmented Reality (AR) and Virtual Reality (VR)

"Virtual Reality was once the dream of science fiction. But the internet was also once a dream, and so were computers and smartphones. The future is coming."
— Mark Zuckerberg

A s we stand on the brink of a new era of digital engagement, Augmented Reality (AR) and Virtual Reality (VR) emerge not merely as technological innovations but as transformative forces reshaping the very essence of customer interaction and business innovation. This chapter ventures deep into the realms of AR and VR, shedding light on their capacity to revolutionize industries by offering immersive experiences that transcend the traditional boundaries of physical and digital realms. By exploring the foundational aspects of AR and VR, alongside their diverse applications, we aim to provide entrepreneurs with a roadmap to harness these technologies for creating ventures that are not only cutting-edge but also deeply resonant with their audiences.

The transformative journey of AR and VR from niche technologies to mainstream tools of engagement offers a glimpse into the future of entrepreneurship—one where immersive experiences become the norm, enabling businesses to connect with their customers in more meaningful and impactful ways. Through detailed exploration, this chapter highlights how AR and VR can serve as powerful mediums for storytelling, customer engagement, and even operational efficiency, pushing the envelope of what's possible in digital innovation.

Furthermore, this exploration into AR and VR delves into the strategic considerations necessary for integrating these technologies into business models. It underscores the importance of thoughtful application, user-centric design, and the potential of AR and VR to not just enhance the way businesses interact with their customers but to also solve complex challenges in novel and effective ways. Entrepreneurs are encouraged to view AR and VR not just as tools but as gateways to building richer, more engaging customer experiences that stand the test of time.

Opening Anecdote: The Virtual Try-On Revolution in Fashion

In the fashion industry, AR has bridged the gap between online shopping's convenience and the desire for a tangible try-on experience. Brands like Warby Parker and Sephora have implemented AR technology to allow customers to virtually try on glasses and makeup from the comfort of their homes, significantly enhancing the online shopping experience and reducing return rates.

> *Quick Thought:*
> *AR and VR represent more than technological advancements; they are gateways to creating deeply personalized and immersive experiences that connect with users on an unprecedented level.*

Entrepreneurship in Action: Key Ingredients

- **User-Centric Design:** Crafting AR and VR experiences that are intuitive, engaging, and tailored to the user's needs and context.
- **Innovative Applications:** Exploring beyond conventional use cases to discover unique ways AR and VR can solve problems, enhance experiences, and create value.
- **Strategic Integration:** Seamlessly integrating AR and VR into your business strategy to complement and enhance your product offerings, marketing efforts, and customer service.

Case Study: Virtual Real Estate Tours with Matterport

Background:

Matterport has revolutionized the real estate industry by offering 3D virtual tour solutions. By creating detailed digital twins of properties, Matterport enables prospective buyers to explore homes and commercial spaces in immersive virtual reality, transcending geographical constraints and time limitations.

Approach:

Utilizing advanced 3D scanning technology, Matterport captures high-quality imagery of physical spaces to construct accurate virtual models. These models are then accessible via VR headsets, providing an immersive viewing experience that closely mimics an in-person visit.

Solution:

Matterport's platform not only aids real estate marketing but also enhances the decision-making process for buyers, allowing for a thorough exploration of properties without physical presence. This technology has applications in architecture, interior design, and construction, offering a powerful tool for visualization and planning.

Impact:

Matterport's success illustrates how AR and VR can transform traditional industries by offering innovative solutions to longstanding challenges. It demonstrates the potential for immersive technologies to enhance customer experiences and streamline operations.

Pro Tip: Balance Immersion with Accessibility: When developing AR and VR experiences, strive for a balance between immersive depth and user accessibility. Consider the diversity of your audience's technology access and comfort levels with new technologies. By designing experiences that are both captivating and accessible, you ensure broader adoption and a more inclusive approach to innovation.

Exercise: Immersive Experience Design Challenge

1. Exploration and Ideation:

- **Identify Pain Points:** Look for challenges within your business or industry where AR or VR could offer a novel solution.
- **Creative Brainstorming:** Organize a brainstorming session focused on generating innovative AR/VR solutions to these challenges.
- **Concept Selection:** Evaluate the ideas based on feasibility, potential impact, and alignment with your business goals, selecting the most promising concept to develop further.

2. Development and Prototyping:

- **Rapid Prototyping:** Create a prototype of your AR/VR solution, focusing on core functionality and user experience.
- **User Testing:** Conduct user testing sessions to gather feedback on the usability, effectiveness, and engagement of your prototype.
- **Iterative Improvement:** Refine your prototype based on feedback, focusing on enhancing the user experience and solving the identified pain points effectively.

3. Launch and Iteration:

- **Market Introduction:** Develop a strategy for introducing your AR/VR solution to the market, considering target audiences, marketing channels, and launch timing.

- **Performance Monitoring:** After launch, closely monitor user engagement and solution performance, collecting data to inform future iterations.
- **Continuous Evolution:** Stay attuned to technological advancements in AR and VR, ready to adapt and evolve your solution to leverage new capabilities and enhance user experiences.

Challenge For You:

Imagine transforming one aspect of your customer's journey using AR or VR to create a more engaging, informative, or immersive experience. Sketch out this transformed journey, detailing the touchpoints enhanced by AR/VR, the technology implementation, and the expected outcomes. Reflect on how this integration could elevate your brand experience and deepen customer connections.

Conclusion:

This chapter has journeyed through the transformative landscapes of AR and VR, highlighting their capacity to revolutionize business practices, product offerings, and customer experiences. As we venture further into the era of immersive technologies, AR and VR stand out as essential tools for entrepreneurs seeking to innovate, engage, and captivate in an increasingly digital world.

Embracing these technologies with creativity, strategic insight, and a commitment to user-centered design will position entrepreneurial ventures at the forefront of the next wave of digital transformation. As we continue to explore the impact of emerging technologies, let AR and VR inspire you to reimagine the boundaries of what's possible, creating experiences that were once the stuff of dreams.

7

Cybersecurity and Data Privacy

"Privacy is not something that I'm merely entitled to, it's an absolute prerequisite."
— Marlon Brando

The digital era ushers in unparalleled opportunities for growth and innovation, yet it also brings to the forefront the critical challenges of cybersecurity and data privacy. As businesses navigate the complexities of the online world, the imperative to protect sensitive information becomes increasingly paramount, resonating with Marlon Brando's emphasis on privacy as a foundational necessity. This chapter aims to demystify the intricacies of cybersecurity and data privacy, shedding light on their vital importance for entrepreneurs who are steering their ventures through the digital landscape.

With the advent of sophisticated cyber threats, the responsibility of securing digital assets extends beyond the IT department to become a cornerstone of business strategy and operations. This narrative explores the essential practices and frameworks that can empower entrepreneurs to fortify their digital fortresses, ensuring the integrity of customer data and the continuity of their operations. By embedding a culture of security and privacy within their ventures, entrepreneurs can not only navigate the digital terrain with confidence but also cultivate trust among their customers and stakeholders.

Moreover, this exploration delves into the evolving legal landscape surrounding data protection, offering insights into how businesses can remain compliant with global regulations while championing the cause of digital privacy. Through a holistic approach that integrates risk management, technological innovation, and ethical considerations, this chapter provides a blueprint for entrepreneurs to harness the power of cybersecurity and data privacy as catalysts for sustainable growth and competitive advantage.

Opening Anecdote: The Target Data Breach Reckoning

In 2013, Target suffered a massive data breach that compromised the personal information of millions of customers. This incident not only led to significant financial losses and legal consequences for the retail giant but also eroded consumer trust. It serves as a stark reminder of the cybersecurity risks businesses face and the importance of robust security measures to protect sensitive data.

> *Quick Thought:*
> *Cybersecurity and data privacy are not just IT issues; they are strategic business imperatives that require a*

proactive, integrated approach to protect assets, maintain customer trust, and ensure business continuity.

Entrepreneurship in Action: Key Ingredients

- **Proactive Risk Management:** Anticipating potential cybersecurity threats and vulnerabilities and taking pre-emptive actions to mitigate risks.
- **Culture of Security Awareness:** Cultivating a workplace where every employee is aware of cybersecurity best practices and their role in safeguarding the company's digital assets.
- **Adherence to Legal and Ethical Standards:** Ensuring compliance with global data protection regulations and ethical standards to protect customer privacy and build trust.

Case Study: Sony's Cybersecurity Evolution

Background:

Following a high-profile cyberattack in 2014, Sony Pictures Entertainment embarked on a comprehensive overhaul of its cybersecurity posture. The attack highlighted the need for stronger defenses and a more resilient digital infrastructure.

Approach:

Sony instituted a multi-layered security strategy that encompassed enhanced encryption, rigorous access controls, and continuous monitoring of its digital ecosystem. The company also prioritized cybersecurity awareness among its employees, embedding security consciousness into the corporate culture.

Solution:

The transformation included deploying state-of-the-art cybersecurity technologies, establishing a dedicated cyber incident response team, and fostering collaborations with external cybersecurity experts and law enforcement agencies.

Impact:

Sony's proactive measures have significantly fortified its defenses against cyber threats, minimizing vulnerabilities and setting a new standard for corporate cybersecurity resilience. This case illustrates the importance of continuous improvement and adaptation in the face of evolving cyber threats.

```
Pro Tip: Embrace Encryption: Implement encryption as
a fundamental layer of your cybersecurity and data
privacy strategy. Whether it's data at rest, in
transit, or during processing, encryption acts as a
critical barrier, protecting sensitive information
from unauthorized access and breaches.
```

Exercise: Cybersecurity and Data Privacy Deep Dive

1. Cybersecurity Fundamentals Workshop:

- **Identify Threats:** List the top three cybersecurity threats your business might face. Research and document how these threats operate and their potential impact.
- **Analyze Defenses:** For each identified threat, outline three specific defensive measures or technologies you can implement to protect your business.

- **Develop a Response Scenario:** Create a detailed response plan for a hypothetical cybersecurity incident, including initial detection, containment strategies, and communication protocols.

2. Data Privacy Compliance Challenge:

- **Regulatory Research:** Identify three key data protection regulations relevant to your business. Summarize their main requirements and implications for your operations.
- **Compliance Audit:** Conduct a mock audit of your current data handling practices against the requirements of these regulations. Identify three areas of non-compliance or risk.
- **Improvement Plan:** For each area of risk identified in your audit, devise three concrete steps or changes to achieve compliance and enhance data privacy protection.

3. Building a Culture of Cybersecurity Awareness:

- **Awareness Campaign Design:** Plan a three-part cybersecurity awareness campaign for your employees. Include topics like phishing awareness, secure password practices, and safe internet usage.
- **Interactive Training Modules:** Create outlines for three interactive training modules that engage employees in cybersecurity best practices, incorporating quizzes, simulations, and real-life case studies.
- **Evaluation and Feedback:** Develop a three-step process for evaluating the effectiveness of your cybersecurity training program, including feedback surveys, knowledge assessments, and incident response drills.

Challenge For You:

Craft a scenario where your business faces a sophisticated phishing attack. Outline the steps your team takes from detection to resolution, including communication strategies, technical responses, and post-incident analysis. This exercise will help you think critically about your incident response plan and areas for enhancement.

Conclusion:

This chapter has underscored the paramount importance of cybersecurity and data privacy for entrepreneurial ventures, highlighting strategies for risk mitigation, best practices for data protection, and the necessity of fostering a security-aware culture. By prioritizing these elements, entrepreneurs not only safeguard their operations but also reinforce their reputation and customer trust in an increasingly digital world.

As we proceed, we remain committed to exploring the synergy between emerging technologies and entrepreneurial success, ever mindful of the foundational role of cybersecurity and privacy in this dynamic equation.

8

Industry-Specific Technology Trends

*"Technology, used correctly, allows us to amplify human
potential and create opportunities that did not exist before."*
— Ginni Rometty

The landscape of modern industries is being continuously reshaped by the advent of cutting-edge
technologies, propelling businesses into a future where
adaptability and innovation hold the keys to success. This
chapter ventures into the heart of industry-specific technology
trends, shedding light on the transformative impact of these
advancements across a spectrum of sectors. From healthcare
revolutionized by telemedicine to manufacturing transformed
through the Internet of Things (IoT), technology is not only
driving efficiency and sustainability but also redefining the very
fabric of industry operations and customer interactions.

With each industry facing its unique challenges and opportunities, the strategic adoption of technology becomes imperative
for entrepreneurs aiming to carve out competitive advantages
and pioneer new paths. Whether it's leveraging artificial

intelligence (AI) for personalized customer experiences or employing blockchain for enhanced security and transparency, understanding and harnessing these trends is crucial. This chapter aims to equip you with the insights and frameworks to navigate the technological waves shaping your industry, ensuring your venture not only survives but thrives in the digital era.

By examining the pivotal role of technologies tailored to specific industry needs, we illuminate how entrepreneurs can unlock novel solutions and create value in unprecedented ways. The journey through the evolving technological landscape is marked by the potential to amplify human potential and open doors to opportunities that were once beyond reach. As we delve deeper, we also consider the broader implications of these technologies, from ethical considerations to their impact on society and the environment, fostering a holistic view of tech adoption in business.

Opening Anecdote: Revolutionizing Agriculture with Precision Farming

Precision agriculture represents a significant leap forward in farming efficiency and sustainability. By utilizing drones for aerial imaging, sensors for soil and crop monitoring, and big data analytics for informed decision-making, companies like John Deere and more specifically it's subsidiary Blue River Technology, are enabling farmers to increase yields while minimizing resource usage. This approach exemplifies how industry-specific technology can lead to revolutionary changes in traditional practices.

> ### *Quick Thought:*
> *Embracing industry-specific technology trends requires a deep understanding of your sector's unique challenges and opportunities. It's about leveraging technology not just for the sake of innovation, but to genuinely enhance operations, customer experiences, and ultimately, human life.*

Entrepreneurship in Action: Key Ingredients

- **Sector Savvy:** A thorough understanding of your industry's landscape, including regulatory, environmental, and competitive challenges.
- **Technological Agility:** The ability to quickly adopt and adapt to new technologies that offer strategic advantages within your industry.
- **Innovation Focus:** A commitment to exploring and implementing solutions that drive efficiency, enhance customer satisfaction, and open new revenue streams.

Case Study: Revolutionizing Patient Care with Wearable Technology

Background:

In the healthcare sector, wearable technology has become a cornerstone for innovative patient care, offering continuous health monitoring and real-time data collection outside traditional clinical settings.

Approach:

Companies like Fitbit and Apple have integrated health monitoring features into their wearable devices, enabling users to track their physical activity, heart rate, and even detect irregular heart rhythms. These technologies empower individuals with insights into their health and provide valuable data to healthcare providers for personalized care plans.

Solution:

The integration of wearable technology into patient care has facilitated a shift towards preventive medicine, where health issues can be identified and addressed before they escalate into more serious conditions.

Impact:

This shift not only improves individual health outcomes but also reduces the burden on healthcare systems by decreasing the need for in-patient care and intervention.

```
Pro Tip: Customize Tech to Your Industry's Needs:
When integrating new technologies into your business,
tailor your approach to address the specific needs
and pain points of your industry. Look beyond general
benefits and focus on how the technology can solve
sector-specific challenges, enhance customer
experiences, and create a competitive edge.
```

Exercise: Industry Innovation Blueprint

1. Trend Analysis and Application:

- **Spotting Trends:** Identify three emerging technology

trends within your industry and research their current applications and potential impact.

- **Opportunity Mapping:** For each trend, outline three opportunities for application within your business operations or product/service offerings.
- **Barrier Identification:** Identify potential barriers to implementing these technologies and brainstorm three solutions for overcoming each barrier.

2. Customer-Centric Technology Integration:

- **Needs Assessment:** Conduct a survey or focus group to understand your customers' needs and how technology can address them.
- **Solution Design:** Design a technology solution for one of the identified customer needs, ensuring it aligns with industry trends and your business capabilities.
- **Prototype Testing:** Develop a prototype of the solution and test it with a small group of customers, gathering feedback for refinement.

3. Strategic Technology Adoption Plan:

- **Roadmap Development:** Create a strategic roadmap for adopting one of the identified technology trends, including milestones, KPIs, and resource allocation.
- **Change Management:** Develop a change management plan to facilitate the adoption process, addressing employee training, cultural shifts, and stakeholder engagement.
- **Impact Evaluation:** Outline a plan for measuring the impact of the technology adoption on your business, including

performance metrics, customer feedback, and ROI analysis.

Challenge For You:

Envision a future scenario where your business has fully integrated the most impactful technology trend identified in your analysis. Describe how this integration has transformed your operations, customer interactions, and market position. Reflect on the steps needed to realize this vision and the potential challenges along the way.

Conclusion:

This chapter has taken a deep dive into the realm of industry-specific technology trends, showcasing how tailored innovations can significantly impact various sectors. By understanding and strategically integrating these technologies, entrepreneurs can not only stay competitive but also drive meaningful advancements in their industries.

As we move to conclude our exploration, the next chapter will offer reflections and actionable insights on embracing technological trends to chart a successful path forward in the dynamic landscape of entrepreneurship.

9

Harnessing Emerging Technologies for Innovation

*"The future belongs to those who believe in the beauty
of their dreams."*
— Eleanor Roosevelt

Embarking on a journey through the evolving landscape of digital innovation, entrepreneurs stand on the brink of a new era defined by the power of emerging technologies. This chapter unveils the vast potential these technologies hold for transforming business landscapes, driving unparalleled innovation, and crafting solutions that offer profound value to customers and society alike. It's a testament to the notion that with the right technological tools, entrepreneurs can sculpt futures that once dwelled solely in the realm of dreams.

At the core of this exploration is the conviction that emerging technologies are not merely disruptors; they are enablers of a brighter, more inclusive future. By delving into the applications of blockchain, artificial intelligence, the Internet of Things, and beyond, this chapter guides entrepreneurs on how to strategically harness these innovations. It aims to illuminate the path for integrating technology in ways that align with business goals, address pressing challenges, and open doors to new possibilities for growth and impact.

The journey through the terrain of emerging technologies is as much about ethical deployment and sustainable practices as it is about innovation. It challenges entrepreneurs to consider the broader implications of their technological choices, fostering solutions that not only drive economic success but also contribute positively to societal progress and environmental stewardship. Through a narrative that intertwines technological potential with a vision for a better future, this chapter equips entrepreneurs with the knowledge and inspiration to leverage technology in their quest to make a meaningful difference in the world.

Opening Anecdote: Revolutionizing Accessibility with Voice AI

Voice-powered AI technologies are breaking down barriers and revolutionizing accessibility. For instance, Voiceitt, an innovative startup, has developed a voice recognition software that understands non-standard speech patterns, empowering individuals with speech impairments to interact with voice-activated devices. This breakthrough showcases how emerging technologies can address real-world challenges and open up new possibilities for inclusion and accessibility.

Quick Thought:

Innovation through emerging technologies is not just about disruption or efficiency; it's about envisioning and realizing a future where technology amplifies human capabilities and addresses societal challenges.

Entrepreneurship in Action: Key Ingredients

- **Visionary Leadership:** The foresight to recognize the potential of emerging technologies and the courage to pursue new avenues of innovation.
- **Customer-Centric Innovation:** Leveraging technology to solve real problems, enhance customer experiences, and meet unarticulated needs.
- **Agile Experimentation:** The willingness to experiment, fail fast, and iterate, fostering a culture of innovation that embraces risk and learns from setbacks.

Case Study: Transforming Agriculture with AI-Driven Insights

Background:

The integration of AI into agriculture is enabling farmers to make data-driven decisions, optimize resources, and boost crop yields. CropX, an agtech company, utilizes AI and IoT technologies to analyze soil data and provide farmers with actionable insights for irrigation management.

Approach:

By combining advanced soil sensors with AI algorithms, CropX offers a platform that monitors soil conditions, predicts water needs, and optimizes irrigation schedules, ensuring water is used efficiently and crops receive precise care.

Solution:

The CropX system demonstrates how AI can transform traditional farming practices, leading to more sustainable agriculture, reduced water usage, and increased productivity.

Impact:

This innovation not only benefits farmers by increasing operational efficiency and crop yields but also contributes to environmental sustainability by conserving water and reducing waste.

```
Pro Tip: Collaborate to Innovate: Emerging
technologies often require interdisciplinary
knowledge and expertise. Don't hesitate to
collaborate with technology providers, academic
institutions, and industry partners to explore
innovative applications and co-create solutions.
Collaboration can accelerate development, provide
access to specialized knowledge, and open up new
markets.
```

Exercise: Emerging Technologies Exploration

1. Technology Scouting and Ideation:

- **Identify Emerging Tech:** Research and list three emerging technologies with potential applications in your industry.
- **Ideation Workshop:** Host an ideation session to brain-

storm innovative ways these technologies could be applied to solve industry-specific challenges or create new customer experiences.

- **Concept Development:** Choose the most promising idea and develop a concept outline, detailing the technology application, target market, and value proposition.

2. Prototype and Validation:

- **Build a Prototype:** Develop a basic prototype or MVP (Minimum Viable Product) that incorporates the chosen technology to address the selected challenge or opportunity.
- **User Testing:** Conduct a series of user tests to gather feedback on the prototype's usability, effectiveness, and potential impact.
- **Iterative Refinement:** Refine your prototype based on feedback, focusing on enhancing functionality, user experience, and overall value.

3. Strategic Implementation Plan:

- **Market Analysis:** Conduct a comprehensive market analysis to understand the competitive landscape and identify potential barriers to entry.
- **Roadmap Creation:** Develop a detailed implementation roadmap, including key milestones, resource allocation, and go-to-market strategy.
- **Impact Assessment:** Establish metrics and KPIs to assess the impact of the technology implementation on your business and customers.

Challenge For You:

Imagine your venture five years from now, having successfully integrated and capitalized on one of the emerging technologies discussed. Describe how this technology has transformed your business operations, customer engagement, and competitive positioning. Reflect on the strategic steps needed to achieve this vision and the potential hurdles along the way.

Conclusion:

This chapter has highlighted the power of emerging technologies as drivers of innovation and transformation. By embracing these technologies, entrepreneurs can unlock new opportunities, redefine customer experiences, and lead their ventures into a future where technology and human aspiration converge to create extraordinary value.

As we approach the conclusion of our exploration, the next chapter will provide a roadmap for integrating these insights and technologies into your entrepreneurial journey, ensuring you are well-equipped to navigate the dynamic landscape of innovation and opportunity.

10

Future Trends and Predictions

"The best way to predict the future is to invent it."
— Alan Kay

Navigating the cusp of technological revolution, the future unfurls a tapestry rich with innovation, beckoning entrepreneurs to weave new narratives of progress and transformation. As we venture into the future in this concluding chapter, we chart the course of technology trends that promise to reshape the way we live, work, and interact. It's a narrative that positions entrepreneurs as architects of the future, equipped with the foresight and creativity to harness emerging technologies for groundbreaking ventures that push the boundaries of possibility.

In this exploration, we delve into the realms of artificial intelligence, quantum computing, and sustainable tech, among others, to uncover how these forces are driving a paradigm shift across industries. This journey is not just about tracking technological evolution; it's about identifying the opportunities these advancements present for creating more efficient, inclusive, and sustainable business practices. By weaving these technologies into the fabric of their ventures, entrepreneurs can craft solutions that not only meet the demands of the present but also anticipate the needs of the future.

This chapter challenges entrepreneurs to think beyond conventional limits, to envision a world transformed by technology where innovation serves as a bridge to a more equitable and prosperous society. It calls for a blend of visionary thinking, strategic planning, and ethical consideration, urging entrepreneurs to consider the wider implications of their technological choices. As the final chapter of our exploration, it serves as a capstone to the journey we've undertaken together, aiming to equip innovators with the insight and inspiration needed to lead the charge in this dynamic landscape of technological advancement. As we close this book, remember that the future isn't a distant realm to be predicted but a canvas to be painted with the bold strokes of today's innovations.

Opening Anecdote: The Dawn of Autonomous Mobility

The quest for autonomous vehicles represents a fusion of AI, IoT, and robotics, illustrating the dynamic interplay of emerging technologies. Companies like Tesla and Waymo are at the forefront, testing and refining these technologies to bring about a future where transportation is safer, more efficient, and accessible. This endeavor exemplifies the transformative potential of harnessing technological advancements to address complex societal challenges.

Quick Thought:

Staying abreast of technological trends is not merely about adapting to changes; it's about actively participating in the creation of a future where technology amplifies human capabilities, fosters sustainable growth, and opens up new vistas of opportunity.

Entrepreneurship in Action: Key Ingredients

- **Foresight:** The ability to anticipate technological shifts and understand their potential impact on industries and society.
- **Adaptability:** The readiness to pivot and evolve business models in response to emerging technological landscapes.
- **Innovative Leadership:** Cultivating a culture that encourages experimentation, embraces risk-taking, and continuously seeks to leverage technology for meaningful impact.

Case Study: Revolutionizing Healthcare with CRISPR Technology

Background:

CRISPR technology, a groundbreaking gene-editing tool, has the potential to transform medical treatment, enabling precise modifications to DNA to correct genetic defects and treat diseases at their source.

Approach:

Biotech startups like CRISPR Therapeutics are pioneering the application of this technology in clinical settings, targeting conditions like sickle cell disease and beta-thalassemia. By collaborating with researchers, clinicians, and regulatory bodies, these companies are navigating the complex path from scientific discovery to therapeutic application.

Solution:

Through clinical trials and rigorous testing, CRISPR-based therapies are demonstrating their potential to offer lasting cures for previously intractable diseases, heralding a new era in personalized medicine.

Impact:

The advancements in gene editing exemplify how deep scientific knowledge combined with entrepreneurial vision can lead to innovations that fundamentally alter healthcare paradigms, offering hope to millions affected by genetic disorders.

```
Pro Tip: Embrace Interdisciplinary Innovation: The
future of technology and innovation lies at the
intersection of disciplines. Entrepreneurs should
foster interdisciplinary collaboration, combining
insights from science, engineering, design, and
business to create holistic solutions that address
complex challenges in novel ways.
```

Exercise: Future-Ready Innovation Plan

1. Trend Mapping and Scenario Planning:

- **Identify Emerging Trends:** Research and document three emerging technological trends that have the potential to impact your industry.

- **Develop Scenarios:** For each trend, outline three potential future scenarios, including both opportunities and challenges these trends might present.
- **Strategic Responses:** Craft strategic responses for navigating each scenario, focusing on innovation, adaptation, and resilience.

2. Technology Adoption Roadmap:

- **Assessment:** Evaluate your current technology stack and identify gaps in relation to future trends.
- **Roadmap Creation:** Develop a technology adoption roadmap, prioritizing technologies that align with your strategic goals and future scenarios.
- **Implementation Plan:** Outline actionable steps for technology implementation, including timelines, resource allocation, and key milestones.

3. Leadership and Culture Transformation:

- **Cultivating a Future-Focused Mindset:** Implement leadership development programs that emphasize forward-thinking, innovation, and adaptability.
- **Fostering a Culture of Innovation:** Develop initiatives to cultivate an organizational culture that values continuous learning, experimentation, and technological exploration.
- **Engaging with Ecosystems:** Build relationships with technology partners, startups, and research institutions to stay connected with the innovation ecosystem and leverage external expertise.

Challenge For You:

Imagine it's the year 2040, and your venture has successfully navigated the technological transformations discussed. Write a reflective piece on the strategic decisions, innovations, and adaptations that were pivotal to your success. Consider the impact of these actions on your business model, industry positioning, and societal contribution.

Conclusion:

As we conclude this exploration of future trends and predictions, it's clear that the journey of innovation is both challenging and exhilarating. By understanding emerging technologies, entrepreneurs can not only anticipate the future but actively shape it. The next chapter, and the final one in this series, offers a synthesis of insights and actionable strategies for entrepreneurs ready to embark on this transformative journey, leveraging technology and innovation to forge new paths to success.

Epilogue: Embracing Technology and Innovation: A Journey of Entrepreneurial Success

As we close the chapters of "Future Focused: Mastering Tech and Innovation for the Entrepreneur in the Evolving Business World," we stand on the brink of a future teeming with boundless possibilities. This exploration has not only traversed the current technological landscape but also illuminated the pathways that emerging technologies are carving across various industries.

Recap of Key Takeaways and Insights from the Book:

This journey has underscored the transformative power of digital transformation, showcasing businesses that have redefined their domains through strategic technology adoption. From Amazon's and Netflix's reimagining of consumer experiences to Spotify's personalized content delivery powered by AI, we've seen how embracing technological innovation propels businesses forward. The Internet of Things (IoT), with its promise of interconnected efficiency, and the groundbreaking potential of blockchain for secure, transparent transactions, have been highlighted as key drivers of industry evolution. Additionally, the immersive realms of AR and VR have opened new vistas for customer engagement, while the imperative of cybersecurity and data privacy has been established as foundational to maintaining trust and integrity in a digital-first world.

Encouraging Ongoing Learning and Adaptation:

The trajectory of technology and innovation is ever-evolving, with each breakthrough and adaptation laying the groundwork for the next leap forward. In this dynamic environment, the entrepreneurial spirit is characterized by an insatiable curiosity and an unwavering commitment to continuous learning. Embrace this journey of perpetual discovery, where each technological advancement presents an opportunity to refine your strategies, enhance your offerings, and deepen your understanding of the markets you serve.

Empowering Entrepreneurs to Drive Technological Adoption:

In the tapestry of technological progress, entrepreneurs are the weavers, integrating threads of innovation into the fabric of business to create something truly transformative. Your role extends beyond adopting technology; it involves leading the charge in reimagining how these tools can solve existing challenges, unlock new opportunities, and redefine what's possible. Whether through the strategic application of AI and ML, the operational efficiencies gained from IoT, or the trust established through blockchain, your vision and actions today are shaping the business landscape of tomorrow.

Embracing the Future with Confidence and Creativity:

As we look to the horizon, the future of technology and innovation is replete with potential—ready to be shaped by visionary entrepreneurs who dare to dream and do. The journey ahead will undoubtedly present challenges, but with resilience, creativity, and a forward-thinking mindset, these obstacles become the stepping stones to unparalleled success.

Conclusion:

"Future Focused" has aimed to be more than just a compendium of insights; it seeks to be a catalyst for action—a guide that empowers you to harness the power of technology and innovation in your entrepreneurial endeavors. As you move forward, let the principles of adaptability, innovation, and visionary leadership guide your path. The future is not a distant dream; it is being created today, with each decision you make and each innovation you embrace.

In crafting this volume, the goal has been to share knowledge and inspire action, equipping you with the tools and perspectives needed to navigate the ever-changing technological landscape. It is with hope and anticipation that this book serves not only as a resource but as an inspiration, encouraging you to explore, innovate, and lead in the age of technology and innovation.

As we part ways, may your journey be marked by bold exploration, transformative innovation, and enduring success. Here's to the future you will shape—a future bright with the promise of technology and the enduring power of entrepreneurial spirit.

Thank you for embarking on this journey through "Future Focused." May the insights within these pages light your way as you navigate the exciting challenges and opportunities of the tech-driven world.

Bonus Section: Workshop Templates and Resources

This bonus section is designed to empower you, the visionary entrepreneur, with practical tools, insights, and resources necessary for navigating the digital era. By addressing the essential areas of digital transformation, emerging technologies, innovation workshops, AI and ML projects, and cybersecurity, I aim to provide a comprehensive kit that not only educates but enables immediate action.

By empowering yourself with these resources, you're taking a significant step toward leading your business into a future marked by innovation, security, and success.

Note to Readers: Each tool, platform, and resource mentioned is selected for its value and applicability. Where tools offer both free and premium options, I've prioritized those with substantial free offerings. However, we encourage exploring premium features that might be especially beneficial to your specific needs as offers and pricing change regularly.

Digital Transformation Blueprint

The Digital Transformation Blueprint is your strategic plan for integrating digital technology into all areas of your business, fundamentally changing how you operate and deliver value to customers. It's a roadmap for continuous improvement, innovation, and adaptation in a rapidly evolving digital ecosystem.

Blueprint Components:

1. Digital Readiness Assessment Before embarking on a transformation, understanding your current digital maturity is crucial. This assessment evaluates your use of digital tools, team's digital skills, and organizational culture's readiness for change.

How to Use:

- **Assessment Questions:** Start with a set of questions to evaluate your digital readiness. Access McKinsey Digital's insights here (https://www.mckinsey.com/capabilities/mckinsey-digital/how-we-help-clients) for frameworks and thought leadership to guide your assessment. McKinsey offers publications on digital readiness that are freely available and provide valuable perspectives.
- **Scoring System:** Develop a simple scoring system to rate your readiness across key areas: Technology, People, Processes, and Data.

- **Evaluation:** Use the results to identify strengths and gaps, informing your blueprint's focus areas.

2. Vision and Strategy Worksheet Defining a clear vision and strategy for your digital transformation is essential for success.
Guided Steps:

- **Vision Statement:** Articulate what digital transformation will achieve for your company. Consider improvements in customer experience, operational efficiency, or new business models.
- **Strategic Goals:** Break down your vision into strategic goals, such as implementing an omnichannel customer service platform or adopting cloud computing.
- **Action Plan:** Outline actions, responsible teams, and timelines for each goal. Utilize tools like Trello and Asana for planning; both offer free versions suitable for small teams. Visit Trello (**https://trello.com/**) or Asana (**https://asana.com/**) to sign up and start planning.

3. Technology Audit and Selection Framework Evaluating current technology and selecting new solutions is fundamental to digital transformation.
Actionable Framework:

- **Current Technology Audit:** Assess the effectiveness and integration of current technology solutions.
- **Needs Analysis:** Identify needs based on strategic goals, potentially requiring new CRM software, data analytics tools, or cybersecurity solutions.
- **Selection Criteria:** Develop selection criteria focusing

on scalability, security, vendor support, and compatibility. Access Gartner's research for technology selection insights here (**https://www.gartner.com/**). While comprehensive reports may require a subscription, Gartner's blogs and summaries offer valuable free insights.

4. Change Management Plan A successful transformation also requires managing the human element.
Detailed Plan:

- **Stakeholder Analysis:** Identify stakeholders and their attitudes towards digital transformation, including employees, management, and customers.
- **Communication Strategy:** Develop a communication plan using tools like Slack (https://slack.com/) to manage and facilitate discussions. Slack helps address concerns and communicate the benefits of upcoming changes.
- **Training Programs:** Plan for training and upskilling employees with digital literacy programs or software-specific training. Explore Coursera (https://www.coursera.org/) and Udemy (https://www.udemy.com/) for relevant courses, many of which are free or offer the first few lessons at no cost. Direct links to recommended courses can be found in our digital repository's downloadable resources section.

Your Digital Transformation Blueprint is a living document that guides your business through its digital evolution journey. As you implement changes, regularly revisit and update the blueprint to reflect new insights, technological advancements, and shifts in your business environment. This adaptable approach ensures your transformation efforts remain aligned with your business goals and the digital landscape's rapid pace.

Emerging Technologies Exploration Toolkit

Embark on a journey to uncover and harness the potential of emerging technologies with our in-depth Exploration Toolkit. This toolkit is designed to guide entrepreneurs through the vast landscape of new technological frontiers, combining structured worksheets, detailed guides, and practical checklists for maximal impact.

Toolkit Components Explained:

1. Technology Radar Worksheet Your starting point for identifying and categorizing emerging technologies that could influence your industry. This worksheet helps you visually map out the development stage and potential impact of each technology on your business.

How to Use:

- **Technology Identification:** List emerging technologies spotted in your research, industry reports, or from competitors.
- **Current State of Development:** Indicate the stage of each technology (e.g., Concept, Development, Testing, Market Introduction) to gauge its readiness.
- **Potential Impact:** Assess the potential impact on your

business (High, Medium, Low).

- **Application Ideas:** Note how each technology could be applied within your operations or offerings.
- **Resource Link:** For creating a technology radar, consider using tools like Miro (https://miro.com/) which offers a technology radar template to visually organize technologies according to their maturity and your business's interest level.

2. Exploration Guide Template A structured template to systematically research and evaluate the potential applications and implications of each identified technology.

Guided Steps:

- **Overview of the Technology:** Summarize the technology and its current industry applications.
- **Industry Impact Assessment:** Reflect on how the technology could revolutionize or disrupt your industry.
- **Business Application Brainstorm:** Structured prompts to innovate applications within your business.
- **Next Steps Plan:** Outline actionable exploration or adoption steps.
- **Resource Link:** For in-depth technology exploration, CB Insights (https://www.cbinsights.com/) provides reports and analyses on various emerging technologies and industry trends.

3. Partnership and Collaboration Strategy Planner Map out potential partnerships or collaborations to access the needed expertise and resources for technology adoption.

Actionable Framework:

- **Potential Partners List:** Compile potential partners already working with or developing the technologies.
- **Evaluation Criteria:** Criteria such as technological expertise, market presence, and business goal alignment.
- **Engagement Strategy:** Plan for initiating contact and proposing collaboration.
- **Resource Link:** For identifying and connecting with potential partners, Crunchbase (**https://www.crunchbase.com/**) is an excellent resource for finding companies by technology sector and stage.

4. Prototype Development Checklist Guide the transition from theoretical applications to tangible solutions through prototyping, covering all essential bases from setting clear objectives to planning development milestones.

Detailed Checklist:

- **Objective Definition:** Clarify what the prototype aims to achieve.
- **Resource Inventory:** List required resources for the prototype.
- **Feasibility Study:** Steps for a basic feasibility study on market demand and technical viability.
- **Milestone Planning:** Key development milestones for tracking progress.
- **Resource Link:** For prototyping guidance, the Adobe XD Ideas (https://xd.adobe.com/ideas/process/prototyping/) portal offers insights and tools for both digital and physical prototype creation.

Conclusion: This toolkit provides a strategic pathway through the exploratory stages of technological adoption, from initial discovery to prototype development readiness. Each component builds upon the previous, ensuring a comprehensive understanding and strategic approach to leveraging emerging technologies.

Innovative Application Workshop Guide

Unlock the collective creative potential of your team with this detailed guide. Designed to foster innovative thinking and productive discussions, this guide will lead you through organizing and executing successful ideation sessions, complete with techniques for encouraging out-of-the-box thinking and worksheets for developing your most promising ideas.

Guide Components Explained:

1. Organizing Ideation Sessions Start by setting the stage for a successful ideation session with clear goals, participant guidelines, and a conducive environment.

How to Use:

- **Define Objectives:** Clearly articulate the goals of the session. Are you seeking solutions to a specific problem, exploring new product ideas, or looking for ways to improve processes?
- **Select Participants:** Choose a diverse group of participants from various departments to ensure a wide range of perspectives.
- **Prepare the Space:** Create a comfortable and inspiring environment. Consider aspects like room layout, available

tools (e.g., whiteboards, sticky notes), and any virtual collaboration tools if conducting the session remotely.

- **Resource Link:** SessionLab (https://www.sessionlab.co m/) offers an array of resources and templates for planning and executing effective workshops.

2. Facilitating Ideation Sessions Facilitating ideation involves guiding participants through the creative process, from divergent thinking to convergent thinking, ensuring productive and focused discussions.

Guided Steps:

- **Warm-Up Exercises:** Start with quick, creative exercises to loosen up participants and encourage open-mindedness.
- **Idea Generation:** Use techniques like brainstorming, brainwriting, or the SCAMPER method (SCAMPER is an acronym for Substitute, Combine, Adapt, Modify/Magnify, Purpose, Eliminate/Minimize and Rearrange/Reverse) to generate ideas. Encourage all participants to contribute, reminding them that no idea is too "out there."
- **Guiding Discussion:** Keep discussions focused and constructive, encouraging participants to build on each other's ideas.
- **Resource Link:** The IDEO Design Kit (https://www.id eo.com/journal/design-kit-the-human-centered-design-toolkit) provides a wealth of techniques for stimulating creativity and fostering productive ideation sessions.

3. Concept Development Worksheets Capture and refine the most promising ideas from your ideation session with structured worksheets that guide you through evaluating,

enhancing, and selecting concepts for further development.
How to Use:

- **Idea Capture:** Use the worksheet to document all generated ideas, ensuring they are clearly described and attributed.
- **Evaluation Criteria:** Establish criteria for evaluating ideas, such as feasibility, potential impact, and alignment with business goals.
- **Selection Process:** Guide participants through a structured process to select the most promising ideas for further exploration and development.
- **Next Steps:** Outline action items for selected ideas, including assigning responsibilities and setting timelines for prototype development or further research.
- **Resource Link:** For creating and utilizing concept development worksheets, Canva (**https://www.canva.com/**) offers customizable templates that can be adapted for ideation sessions, providing a visual and collaborative platform for capturing and refining ideas.

Conclusion: This Innovative Application Workshop Guide equips you with the methodology and tools to unleash the creative potential within your team or organization. By following these structured steps and leveraging the provided resources, you can foster an environment where groundbreaking ideas flourish and translate into viable, innovative applications that propel your business forward.

AI and ML Innovation Workshop Materials

Step into the future of technology by integrating AI and ML into your business strategies. This section provides non-technical entrepreneurs with a foundational understanding of AI/ML concepts, project planning templates, and guidance on forming strategic partnerships. Each component is designed to demystify these technologies and facilitate their practical application.

Materials Explained:

1. AI/ML Basics Primer Gain a solid understanding of AI and ML, including key terms, concepts, and how they're revolutionizing industries across the globe.

How to Use:

- **Essential Concepts:** Start with the basics of artificial intelligence and machine learning, understanding the difference between the two and their applications. **Artificial Intelligence (AI):** AI mimics human intelligence, enabling machines to perform tasks that typically require human intellect, such as problem-solving and learning. **Machine Learning (ML):** ML, a subset of AI, focuses on building algorithms that allow machines to learn from and make decisions based on data.

- **Terminology:** Get familiar with common terms like algorithms, neural networks, deep learning, natural language processing (NLP), and more. **Algorithms:** Procedures or formulas for solving problems. In AI/ML, algorithms analyze data and make decisions. **Neural Networks:** Computing systems inspired by the human brain's network of neurons. These networks can learn and make decisions independently. **Deep Learning:** An advanced subset of ML using deep neural networks to analyze factors in data, enabling sophisticated capabilities like voice and image recognition. **Natural Language Processing (NLP):** A technology enabling machines to understand and interpret human language.

- **Real-World Applications:** From personalized recommendations on streaming services to autonomous vehicles, AI and ML technologies are behind many innovations you interact with daily. Understanding these applications can inspire potential uses within your own business.

- **Resource Link:** Elements of AI (https://www.elementsofai.com/) offers a free online course that covers AI fundamentals, perfect for entrepreneurs looking to grasp the basics of AI and ML.

2. Project Templates Structured templates guide you through the process of identifying, outlining, and evaluating potential AI/ML initiatives for your business.

How to Use:

- **Initiative Identification:** Use the template to brainstorm potential AI/ML projects, focusing on areas where these technologies could enhance efficiency, customer experience, or innovation.

- **Feasibility Assessment:** Assess the technical feasibility, potential impact, and required resources for each proposed initiative, helping prioritize projects based on business value and implementation viability.
- **Action Plan:** Develop a step-by-step plan for your top-priority AI/ML projects, including milestones, required resources, and potential challenges.
- **Resource Link:** Trello (https://trello.com/) offers a versatile AI project planning template that can be customized for brainstorming and tracking the progress of your AI/ML initiatives.

3. Guide to Partnering with AI/ML Experts and Technology Providers Successfully implementing AI/ML projects often requires collaboration with specialists in the field. This guide helps you navigate the process of finding and working with the right partners.

How to Use:

- **Identifying Potential Partners:** Understand what to look for in AI/ML experts and technology providers, including expertise in your industry, portfolio of successful projects, and compatibility with your business goals.
- **Engagement Strategies:** Learn best practices for reaching out to potential partners, from initial contact to crafting proposals that outline collaboration benefits for both parties.
- **Partnership Management:** Tips for managing the partnership, ensuring clear communication, and aligning

project objectives with your business strategy.

- **Resource Link:** Upwork (https://www.upwork.com/) and Toptal (https://www.toptal.com/) are platforms where you can find freelance AI/ML experts with the specific skills you need to bring your projects to life. Additionally, Crunchbase (https://www.crunchbase.com/) can be a valuable resource for identifying leading AI technology providers and startups.

Conclusion: Leveraging AI and ML technologies in your business doesn't have to be a daunting task. With the right foundation, planning tools, and partnerships, even non-technical entrepreneurs can embark on successful AI/ML initiatives. These workshop materials are designed to provide you with the knowledge and resources needed to navigate the AI/ML landscape confidently, transforming innovative ideas into tangible, value-adding projects.

Cybersecurity and Data Privacy Deep Dive Kit

In today's digital age, the importance of cybersecurity and data privacy cannot be overstated. This Deep Dive Kit provides SMEs with essential tools and knowledge to fortify their defenses, comply with data privacy regulations, and cultivate a security-conscious culture.

Kit Components Detailed:
1. Cybersecurity Checklist for SMEs A comprehensive checklist that guides you through establishing robust cybersecurity measures, from foundational practices to advanced security strategies.
How to Use:

- **Foundation Protocols:** Start with the basics—ensure that firewalls are in place, passwords are strong and regularly updated, and antivirus software is installed and kept current.
- **Employee Training:** Implement regular cybersecurity awareness training for all employees to recognize phishing attempts and other common cyber threats.
- **Access Management:** Limit access to sensitive information and use two-factor authentication wherever possible.

- **Regular Updates:** Keep all software up to date to protect against vulnerabilities.
- **Backup and Recovery:** Establish regular data backup routines and have a clear disaster recovery plan in place.
- **Advanced Threat Protection:** Explore advanced security measures such as encryption, intrusion detection systems, and secure web gateways.
- **Resource Link:** The Federal Communications Commission offers a Cybersecurity Planner (https://www.fcc.gov/cyberplanner) that provides customized recommendations for businesses.

2. Data Privacy Compliance Guide Navigate the complexities of data privacy regulations and ensure your business practices are in full compliance, protecting both your customers' information and your company's reputation.

How to Use:

- **Understand Regulations:** Familiarize yourself with relevant data protection laws (e.g., GDPR in Europe, CCPA in California) that apply to your business.
- **Data Handling Procedures:** Develop clear policies for collecting, storing, processing, and sharing personal data.
- **Consumer Rights:** Implement procedures for responding to consumers' requests regarding their data (e.g., requests for deletion or access to their data).
- **Data Privacy Officer:** Consider appointing a Data Privacy Officer (DPO) to oversee compliance efforts, especially if your business falls under certain criteria outlined in GDPR.
- **Resource Link:** The International Association of Privacy Professionals (IAPP) (https://iapp.org/) provides extensive

resources and guidelines for understanding and implementing data privacy laws.

3. Scenario-Based Cybersecurity Exercises Engage your team in practical exercises designed to simulate real-world cyber threat scenarios, enhancing their ability to respond effectively and minimize potential impacts.

How to Use:

- **Simulate Phishing Attacks:** Use simulated phishing exercises to teach employees how to spot and respond to malicious emails.
- **Breach Response Plan Testing:** Conduct drills to test your team's response to data breaches, including communication strategies and technical responses.
- **Physical Security Breaches:** Run scenarios that involve physical access breaches to sensitive information, reinforcing the importance of secure access controls.
- **Review and Improve:** After each exercise, review performance and identify areas for improvement. Adjust policies and training programs accordingly.
- **Resource Link:** Cybersecurity & Infrastructure Security Agency (CISA) (https://www.cisa.gov/cybersecurity-train ing-exercises) offers exercise programs to help organizations test their preparedness for cyber incidents.

Conclusion: This Cybersecurity and Data Privacy Deep Dive Kit serves as a critical resource for businesses aiming to safeguard their digital assets and ensure data privacy compliance. By systematically implementing the checklist, adhering to the compliance guide, and engaging in scenario-based exercises,

SMEs can build a resilient security posture that protects against cyber threats and upholds customer trust.

Embrace these resources as part of your ongoing commitment to cybersecurity and privacy. In doing so, you not only protect your business but also contribute to a safer, more secure digital ecosystem for all.

Virtual Workshop Facilitator's Guide

Master the art of virtual workshop facilitation with this detailed guide. From leveraging the latest digital tools to fostering an inclusive atmosphere, these insights and resources will help you deliver sessions that are not only productive but also engaging for all participants.

Guide Components Detailed:

1. Virtual Workshop Planning Best Practices Effective planning is the foundation of any successful virtual workshop. These best practices ensure that you're well-prepared to deliver a seamless and impactful session.

How to Use:

- **Technology Checks:** Prior to the workshop, test all technology and platforms to be used. Ensure that all participants have access to and are familiar with these tools.
- **Participant Engagement Strategies:** Plan interactive elements such as polls, Q&A sessions, and breakout discussions to keep participants engaged.
- **Time Management:** Design your agenda with clear time allocations for each segment, including breaks to prevent Zoom fatigue.
- **Pre-Workshop Communication:** Send out agendas, pre-reading materials, and technology guides in advance to help

participants prepare.

- **Resource Link:** Zoom (https://zoom.us/) offers comprehensive guides and tutorials for hosting effective meetings and workshops online, including breakout room management and interactive polls.

2. Templates for Virtual Collaboration Utilize digital tools and templates to facilitate brainstorming, collaboration, and feedback collection during your virtual workshops.

How to Use:

- **Digital Whiteboards:** Platforms like Miro (https://miro.com/) or MURAL (https://www.mural.co/) offer collaborative whiteboard functionality for brainstorming and visual exercises.
- **Brainstorming Apps:** Tools such as Stormboard (https://www.stormboard.com/) help capture and organize ideas in real-time, allowing participants to contribute simultaneously.
- **Feedback Polls:** Use tools like Slido (https://www.sli.do/) or Mentimeter (https://www.mentimeter.com/) to gather instant feedback, run live polls, and engage participants.
- **Resource Link:** Explore the Miroverse Community Templates (https://miro.com/miroverse/) for a wide range of pre-designed workshop and collaboration templates that can be easily integrated into your virtual sessions.

3. Fostering an Inclusive and Interactive Virtual Environment Creating a space where every participant feels valued and heard is essential for the success of your virtual workshop.

How to Use:

- **Inclusive Practices:** Begin with introductions and ice-breakers to create a welcoming atmosphere. Use features like "hand raising" and encourage the use of chat for questions and comments to ensure everyone can contribute.
- **Engagement Techniques:** Rotate speaking roles, facilitate small group discussions in breakout rooms, and use engagement tools to maintain interest and participation.
- **Accessibility Considerations:** Ensure that your workshop is accessible to all participants, including those with disabilities. This might involve providing captioning for content or choosing platforms that are compliant with accessibility standards.
- **Follow-Up:** After the workshop, send out a summary of the session, along with any action items, additional resources, and a feedback survey to gather insights for improvement.
- **Resource Link:** The Association for Talent Development (ATD) (https://www.td.org/) offers resources and courses on engaging and inclusive training practices that can enhance your virtual facilitation skills.

Conclusion: This Virtual Workshop Facilitator's Guide equips you with the strategies, tools, and techniques needed to lead successful online sessions. By focusing on meticulous planning, leveraging digital collaboration tools, and fostering an inclusive environment, you can ensure that your virtual workshops are as engaging and effective as in-person sessions. Embrace these practices to elevate your facilitation skills and deliver memorable, impactful virtual workshops.

The Ask

Dear Innovators and Trailblazers,

As we wrap up "Future Focused: Mastering Tech and Innovation for the Entrepreneur in the Evolving Business World," I hope it has fueled your enthusiasm for innovation and provided you with the insights to navigate the tech landscape with confidence. This guide was crafted to be your beacon, illuminating the path to harnessing emerging technologies for entrepreneurial triumph.

If "Future Focused" has sparked your passion and equipped you for the journey ahead, please share your journey with a review on Amazon. Your feedback, whether it's celebrating new discoveries or suggesting avenues for exploration, enriches our collective quest for innovation, guiding fellow entrepreneurs as they embark on their own tech adventures.

For further exploration and to arm yourself with more strategies for a tech-driven future, I invite you to explore my Amazon author page (https://www.amazon.com/author/patrickhperrine). Together, we can foster a community of visionary entrepreneurs, each review and shared insight kindling the spirit of innovation for future disruptors.

Onward to Innovation,
Patrick

About the Author

Patrick H. Perrine is a trailblazing author, mentor, and seasoned entrepreneur with a spirit that exemplifies the essence of entrepreneurship. From his humble beginnings as a paperboy in Minnesota to his emergence as a globally recognized industry leader, his journey epitomizes resilience and determination.

Fueled by an insatiable thirst for knowledge, Patrick opted for university over his senior high school year, setting the stage for his relentless pursuit of personal growth. His tenure with UpStart, an organization championing educational opportunities for first-generation Americans, ignited his lifelong commitment to empowering others, extending beyond business and into his early philanthropic endeavors.

In his twenties, Patrick served as a Founding Board member for The Point Foundation, the largest LGBTQ scholarship foundation today. His dedication to fostering inclusivity and aiding LGBTQ students in higher education continues to positively impact hundreds of lives.

Patrick's entrepreneurial journey took flight with myPartner.com, an online dating service that addressed a critical gap in the market. Recognized as one of the "Best Matchmakers" and "Most Innovative Online Dating Sites" by the iDate Industry, the venture earned a Certificate of Recognition issued by California Legislature Assemblyman Mark Leno. This marked Patrick's first step in a journey filled with identifying unique opportunities and delivering transformative solutions across industries from skincare to dog tech.

Despite the hurdles encountered, Patrick's determination only amplified. His passion for nurturing startups led him to establish Rincon Hill Advisors. During this period, he served as a Steering Committee member for StartOut, a leading nonprofit fostering queer entrepreneurship, and consulted with Fortune 500 companies like Berkshire Hathaway and Intuit.

Adding to his achievements as an entrepreneur, Patrick became an angel investor. His foresight led him to invest in promising startups like MisterB&B, the world's largest gay hotelier, and Roadster, the leading commerce platform for car buying. His dog tech venture, too, gained recognition, leading to his selection as a NGLCC Pitch Finalist and participant in the Seamless IoT Accelerator, earning a $100,000 investment offer as a program graduate.

Most recently, Patrick served as an Entrepreneur in Residence (EiR) with 500 StartUps, an organization committed to uplifting global economies through entrepreneurship. This role solidified his dedication to guiding and uplifting aspiring entrepreneurs.

With a total of six books to his credit, including recent works "Fail Fast, Recover Faster", "Ignite your Dream", and "Fueling the Fire", Patrick continues to share his journey and insights. His writing reflects his unwavering commitment to guiding entrepreneurs through their unique journeys.

Patrick H. Perrine is more than a summary of his accomplishments. He stands as a testament to the power of determination, innovation, and a generous spirit. His contributions have been acknowledged in global press publications such as Forbes, Advocate, and Mirror, but his most profound impact lies in the lives of the entrepreneurs he's guided, inspired, and empowered.

Subscribe to my newsletter:
✉ https://www.patrickperrine.com

Also by Patrick H. Perrine

Your next adventure in entrepreneurship awaits! Choose your guidebook on Amazon (https://www.amazon.com/author/patrickhperrine) or **www.PatrickPerrine.com/books**, and ignite the spark that takes your venture to new heights. The future is yours to shape!

Unicorn Rising: Ascending to the Pinnacle of Entrepreneurship and the Billionaire's Club

Fueled by entrepreneurial dreams and the allure of the Unicorn Club? Patrick H. Perrine is your guide, offering an unparalleled roadmap set to be every entrepreneur's playbook.

"Unicorn Rising" emerges as the cornerstone of the *Be A Unicorn* series, laying the groundwork that "Future Focused" and the other nine volumes build upon.

"Unicorn Rising" is more than a path to towering valuations; it's a compass to innovation, transformative leadership, and sustainable triumph. Dive into leadership's intricacies, the pulse of emerging tech, financial stewardship, and the essence of high-impact entrepreneurship.

However, this isn't a one-size-fits-all roadmap. While Patrick offers foundational wisdom and actionable tools, he accentuates the bespoke nature of each startup's odyssey. Whether you're an entrepreneurial novice or a battle-hardened veteran seeking to recalibrate strategies, this series becomes your beacon.

Embark, defy conventions, and with "Unicorn Rising", elevate to unparalleled entrepreneurial echelons.

Ignite Your Dream: The Quintessential Checklist for Aspiring Entrepreneurs

Ignite Your Dream: The Quintessential Checklist for Aspiring Entrepreneurs" by Patrick H. Perrine is an immersive guide lighting the path towards entrepreneurial success. This power-packed handbook propels you from dreaming to achieving with a carefully curated 100-step map. Dive into real-life entrepreneur stories, extract wisdom, and utilize actionable checklists.

This book transcends theoretical guidelines, providing a mentorship experience designed to turn dreams into reality. Ready to kindle your entrepreneurial spirit? "Ignite your Dream" is your step forward towards unlocking potential and achieving success in the exciting world of entrepreneurship.

Fail Fast, Recover Faster: Bouncing Back From Entrepreneurial Failure

Embrace failure and bounce back stronger with "Fail Fast, Recover Faster: Bouncing Back From Entrepreneurial Failure". It's your guidebook through the tumultuous journey of entrepreneurship, celebrating stumbles as stepping stones towards success. Dive into compelling tales of triumphant entrepreneurs, learn how to pivot rapidly, manage fallout, and convert setbacks into launchpads.

Discover strategies for repairing financial, relationship, and reputation damage, and see your failures as badges of resilience. This transformative book readies you to rebound from failure swiftly, turning your setbacks into your next entrepreneurial triumph. With "Fail Fast, Recover Faster", you're poised to harness your own unicorn moment and turn failure into a launching pad for success.

Fueling the Fire: Nurturing Resilience and Preventing Burnout in Entrepreneurship

In "Fueling the Fire: Nurturing Resilience and Preventing Burnout in Entrepreneurship," seasoned entrepreneur Patrick H. Perrine guides you through the entrepreneurial journey, sharing practical strategies for maintaining resilience and passion. Drawing from 20 years of startup experience, Perrine covers everything from ideation to acquisition.

Discover how to build a support system, manage your time effectively, cultivate a positive work culture, and align your work with your values. Whether you're an experienced entrepreneur or just beginning, "Fueling the Fire" is a must-read for maintaining balance and fulfillment in the dynamic world of entrepreneurship.